CHILDREN'S ROOM

SPOTLIGHT ON NATIVE AMERICANS

APACHE

Wren Richmond

PowerKiDS press

New York

Published in 2016 by The Rosen Publishing Group, Inc.
29 East 21st Street, New York, NY 10010

First Edition

Editor: Karolena Bielecki
Book Design: Kris Everson
Reviewed by: Robert J. Conley, Former Sequoyah Distinguished Professor at Western Carolina University and Director of Native American Studies at Morningside College and Montana State University
Supplemental material reviewed by: Donald A. Grinde, Jr., Professor of Transnational/American Studies at the State University of New York at Buffalo.

Photo Credits: Cover © Don B. Stevenson / Alamy; pp. 4–5 Zack Frank/ Shutterstock.com; pp. 7, 9 North Wind Picture Archives; pp. 8–9 © iStockphoto. com/codyphotography; pp. 11, 14, 17 (right) Peter Newark's American Pictures; p. 13 SuperStock/Getty Images; pp. 17 (left), 19 Corbis; pp. 18, 21, 22, 25, 26, 29 Native Stock; pp. 24–25 Jim Parkin/Shutterstock.com.

Library of Congress Cataloging-in-Publication Data

Richmond, Wren.
  Apache / Wren Richmond.
     pages cm. — (Spotlight on Native Americans)
  Includes bibliographical references and index.
  ISBN 978-1-4994-1666-4 (pbk.)
  ISBN 978-1-4994-1665-7 (6 pack)
  ISBN 978-1-4994-1668-8 (library binding)
  1. Apache Indians—History—Juvenile literature. 2. Apache Indians—Social life and customs—Juvenile literature. I. Title.
  E99.A6R43 2016
  979.004'9725—dc23
                              2015007806

Manufactured in the United States of America

CPSIA Compliance Information: Batch #WS15PK: For Further Information contact Rosen Publishing, New York, New York at 1-800-237-9932

CONTENTS

APACHE HOMELANDS

CHAPTER 1

The Apaches are a North American native people whose historic homeland included a large portion of today's U.S. Southwest and northern Mexico. Today, tens of thousands of Apaches live in the United States, mostly in Oklahoma, New Mexico, and Arizona.

It is uncertain how the Apaches and other Native Americans got to North America. In most native **cultures**, stories of their people's origins have been told for generations. Apache origin stories tell of heroes coming from beneath the earth, led by Changing Woman (or White-painted Woman), who had magic powers. Helped by a spirit known as Life Giver, Changing Woman and other heroes fought monsters and made Earth safe for humans. The stories have great **significance** for Apache culture.

Most scholars believe Apaches migrated from the north, arriving in the Southwest region of today's Arizona and New Mexico perhaps as early as AD 800 or 900. Others think the Apaches might have arrived in the Southwest after the great **drought** of the late 1300s. The drought caused ancient civilizations of the

region, including a people called the Mogollon, to abandon the area and move their farming villages near big rivers. The Apaches would have moved in and replaced them.

In New Mexico, Apaches occupied land that had been abandoned by the ancient Mogollon people, such as these ruins at Gila Cliff Dwellings National Monument.

BEFORE EUROPEAN CONTACT

CHAPTER 2

Before the Spanish began exploring the Southwest in the 1540s, the Eastern Apaches were the lords of the southern Great Plains, with its large herds of buffalo. Mainly a trading people, the Plains Apaches held large annual trade fairs with the Pueblo Indians of New Mexico at the eastern edge of the Great Plains. For several weeks each fall, Apaches from all across the southern Plains traded their buffalo meat and hides to the Pueblos in exchange for corn and pottery.

For the Western Apaches, however, west of the Rio Grande, there were no buffalo herds, only a rugged, desert wasteland that no one else wanted. Here, the Apaches proved themselves one of the most adaptable people in the world. They discovered and harvested the few food plants of the landscape. With so little food, the Apaches spread thinly across the land, living in small, independent units of related families.

It has been estimated that there were once more than 70 million buffalo on the Great Plains. The buffalo provided for many of the Plains Apaches' needs.

Neither the Eastern nor the Western Apaches formed any kind of national government that other nations could do business with. This situation made it impossible for the Spanish, Mexicans, and Americans who later came to the region to enter into treaties with the whole Apache Nation.

THE SPANISH AND MEXICAN ERAS

CHAPTER 3

Beginning with Francisco de Coronado in the 1540s, Spanish explorers in the sixteenth century left accounts of the annual Apache trade fairs with the Pueblo Indians. When the Spanish settled New Mexico in 1598, however, they imposed taxes on the Pueblos that left them without anything to trade with the Apaches. The annual Apache trade fairs came to an end, forever changing the **economy** of the Plains Apaches.

The once-abundant herds of buffalo that roamed the Great Plains were important to the Apaches.

Another huge change came when the Comanche Nation migrated south. Beginning in the early 1700s, they traveled from Wyoming to the southern Great Plains because they wanted to control the southern buffalo herds. Within a few decades, the Comanches drove the Plains Apaches from the area. In about 1724, the Comanches and Apaches fought a great battle on the Plains, which the Apaches lost. Most of the Plains Apaches were driven west, into the mountains of New Mexico. Only two Apache tribes were able to stay on the buffalo plains. The Lipan Apaches stayed south of the Comanches in Texas. The Kiowa-Apaches **allied** with the Kiowa tribe on the Great Plains.

When the Spanish entered the Southwest, they forced the Indians to work for them.

APACHE RAIDS

CHAPTER 4

Indian tribes were forced to adapt dramatically to their new European-American neighbors. The Apaches shifted their economy from buffalo hunting to raiding Spanish ranches. Apaches became so successful at it that the Spanish in northern Mexico complained that they worked all year raising livestock, and suddenly, the Apaches would sweep down from the north and steal them.

Apache raids sometimes occurred hundreds of miles into Mexico. The raiders often went on foot to their target, traveling through the most rugged, isolated **terrain**, avoiding contact with anyone and maintaining the element of surprise.

Striking quickly, the Apaches moved the stolen animals northward at an amazing pace. If the pursuers got too close, some of the Apaches laid ambushes for them, while others continued herding the livestock northward. Once in their home territory, they divided up the livestock and then scattered in small groups. This made pursuing them farther nearly impossible. Apache raiding virtually

Apaches became the most skillful raiders in the history of North America. No one knew when or where they would strike, and catching them was nearly impossible.

halted the advance of Spanish settlement northward from Mexico.

Raiding was so successful that the Apaches had very little reason to attempt to become farmers or ranchers. Even by the late 1800s, the United States had trouble convincing the Apaches to farm or ranch.

HOSTILITIES BETWEEN APACHES AND AMERICANS

CHAPTER 5

In 1848, the United States won a war with Mexico, claiming much of the Apache homeland, including Arizona and New Mexico, which previously belonged to its southern neighbor. Americans began pouring into the region, causing problems for the Apaches because the Americans had little respect for Apache rights to the land.

Over the next 40 years, the Apache groups were rounded up and forced onto **reservations**. Many Apaches, such as the warrior Geronimo, fought against U.S. government troops in defense of their homelands. By the 1880s, however, only some Western Apaches remained outside the reservation system. Even those Apaches confined to reservations often left to wage war in protest over the overcrowding, sickness, and poor food on the reservations.

Finally, in 1886, Geronimo and his small band of followers became the last Apaches to surrender. They were sent to Florida as prisoners of war. Open **hostilities** between Apaches and Americans came to an end, and the reservation era began.

This painting by 19th-century artist Frederic Remington is called *Indian Village Routed, Geronimo Fleeing from Camp.*

13

LIFE ON RESERVATIONS

CHAPTER 6

The U.S. government used the reservation system to try to force Indians to adopt white values. It was a grim time for the Apache people and their culture.

Reservation life was very difficult. Poverty, lack of jobs, despair, and poor food caused serious health problems. Apache populations declined at alarming rates. The population of the Jicarilla Apaches, for example,

Apache children were taken from their families and sent away to harsh boarding schools where they were forbidden to speak their language and dress in Apache clothing.

dropped from 995 in 1905 to only 588 in 1920. By 1920, nearly 90 percent of Jicarilla children suffered from tuberculosis, a serious lung disease.

It was one of the worst periods in American history for Native Americans. They did not have many rights, including freedom of religion. The government was determined to end Indian culture and make Indians just like everyone else, which was a process called acculturation.

These attitudes began to change in the 1930s when Congress passed the Indian Reorganization Act, which allowed the Apaches and other Indian tribes to form tribal governments again. It was not until 1978, however, that the U.S. government passed the American Indian Religious Freedom Act.

Other laws since then have made it easier for tribal governments to operate businesses, which Apache tribes have taken advantage of to improve the lives of their people today.

THE TRADITIONAL APACHE HOME

CHAPTER 7

Apache traditional culture is matrilineal, meaning that a family tree is traced through the mother's family. When an Apache man married, he went to live with his wife's family. Children of the marriage automatically belonged to the wife's **clan**. An Apache mother-in-law was forbidden to talk to her daughter's husband. This helped to avoid conflict in the household.

Apaches lived and traveled most of the year in small units of related families, with little traditional formal government. Leaders were chosen by the others and could lose their position by making foolish or dangerous decisions.

Eastern Apaches lived in **tepees** made of buffalo hides, even after they lost the buffalo plains to the Comanches and had to trade with other Indians to get the hides. Western Apaches, however, invented a structure, called a wickiup, that was perfect for their land. Branches were woven together into a round

(Left) This photo shows an Apache bride dressed for her wedding day. Apache women are respected for their knowledge and hard work. *(Right)* This photo shows Apache chief Antonio Maria with his family in 1897. The family is dressed in their finest clothing for the photograph.

frame and then covered with desert bushes and leaves. Providing shade in the desert heat, the wickiup could be built quickly with materials readily at hand and then quickly abandoned, making the Apaches highly **mobile**. It was also nearly invisible because it blended in so well, making an Apache camp hard to find.

GROWING UP APACHE
CHAPTER 8

Apache children began training in how to survive in their harsh land as soon as they were old enough to walk. Each morning at sunrise, children were sent running to the top of a hill and back. As they grew older, they were required to carry a mouthful of water the whole way without losing any.

On summer mornings, the children would also be made to swim in the ice-cold mountain streams. On winter mornings, they would be made to roll naked in the snow.

Apache girls played with dolls made of cornhusks. The dolls are dressed in leather clothing.

By the time Apache children were teenagers, they had learned to withstand cold, heat, hunger, and thirst that few other humans could endure. They were so **agile** that they could run through their rough terrain farther and faster than soldiers mounted on horseback.

This training produced some the most exceptional **guerrilla warfare** fighters in history. Even as old men, Apache warriors such as Geronimo were superior athletes to the young soldiers who tried to catch them.

Footraces were by far the most important of the Apache sports. Today, this tradition continues as an important part of annual Apache gatherings, most notably among the Jicarilla Apaches in northern New Mexico and the Mescalero Apaches in southeastern New Mexico.

Shown here are Apache babies on cradleboards. The cradleboards left the mother free to perform her work while keeping the babies safe.

APACHE SPIRITUALISM

CHAPTER 9

Apaches never talked about death and never referred to dead people by name. If death was mentioned during the preparations for a war party, the war party would be canceled. Upon the death of a parent, the children's names would be changed so they would not have to recall how the parent had used their name.

When an Apache died, the body was buried as quickly as possible, and the camp was moved. It was believed that illness could be spread by viewing the body or by touching that person's possessions. Everything that person owned was hastily buried with the body.

Apaches also avoided the topic of owls, which they believed were the ghosts of dead people. An owl's hooting caused serious concern in an Apache camp. There were no jokes in the culture regarding owls and no stories about them. Like death, owls were a topic to be avoided.

Today, important Apache ceremonies continue to be performed on reservations, including the Apache Fire Dance and the Mountain Spirit Dance, which celebrate the continuation of Apache culture.

Apache dancers perform the Mountain Spirit Dance in Gallup, New Mexico.

ART AND THE APACHE

CHAPTER 10

Apaches have made important contributions to Native American **scholarship**, literature, and the arts. Jicarilla Apache scholar Veronica E. Velarde Tiller became the first Apache to write a scholarly history of her people, titled *The Jicarilla Apache Tribe*, which

Shown here is a painted hide by Apache artist Joseph Skywolf. Hide paintings were sometimes used to record historic events by the tribe.

concentrates on the problems her people have faced in the twentieth century.

White Mountain Apache poet Roman C. Adrian's poetry has appeared in many publications, including *The Remembered Earth*. The first major collection of Native American literature, this book was published in the late 1960s and is widely used in college courses. The late Chiricahua Apache poet Blossom Haozous published traditional Apache stories in both the Apache language and English, including Apache origin stories. In contrast, Jicarilla Apache creative writers Stacey Velarde and Carson Vicenti write stories about modern life, revealing the problems and joys of being an Indian in today's world.

Mescalero Apache Lorenzo Baca is among the most talented creative artists, working in video, sculpture, art, storytelling, and acting. His "round poems" are circle poems, which are cleverly constructed and fun to read. Baca has been published in several collections of poetry, and he has also made audio recordings.

THE SAN CARLOS RESERVATION TODAY

CHAPTER 11

Most Apaches in Arizona live on reservations. The two biggest Apache reservations, the San Carlos Apache Reservation and the Fort Apache Reservation, are in eastern Arizona. Home to about seven thousand Western Apaches today, the San Carlos Apache Reservation is one of the poorest places in the United States. A quarter of the workforce has no jobs, and 60 percent of the people live in poverty. The tribe lost most of what little farmland it had when part of the reservation was flooded following the building of the Coolidge Dam in 1930.

Tribal members have made some income by mining **semiprecious stones**, such as peridot, and by limited farming. Tourists come to the reservation to hunt, fish, play golf, or gamble. Permits are sold to fishers, hikers, and campers on San Carlos Lake. In early 2015, the San Carlos Apache took on Washington, D.C., lawmakers

Most of San Carlos is harsh, arid land similar to that of the Salt River Canyon shown here.

This statue overlooks the San Carlos Apache golf course in Arizona. The San Carlos Apaches are attempting to increase their income from tourists.

who were working to pass a bill that would give Oak Flat, which is public park space and ceremonial land sacred to the Apache, to a private British copper mining company.

The San Carlos Apache Cultural Center features exhibits on Apache religion and ceremonies. The center also promotes and sells the work of Apache craftspeople.

THE FORT APACHE RESERVATION TODAY

CHAPTER 12

The Fort Apache Reservation in eastern Arizona is home to the Coyotero Apaches and also includes the Cibeque and White Mountain Apaches, a total population of about 9,000.

This photo shows a young Apache girl on horseback at the Fort Apache Reservation.

In 1954, the tribe founded the Fort Apache Recreational Enterprise, leading to much economic activity, including building a ski area and summer resort. The mountains, lakes, and fishing streams attract tourists and their money, boosting tribal income and employment. Permits are sold for white-water rafting, kayaking, and canoeing on Salt River. Farming and cattle raising are also important. The most successful tribal business, however, has been its casino, which lures gamblers by the thousands. The casino opened in 1993 and was so successful it was doubled in size in 1995. The Fort Apache White Mountain Cultural Center is another tourist attraction. It showcases historic Apache objects as well as modern Apache arts and crafts. Outside the center are the old Fort Apache buildings, which were built in 1870, and a re-creation of an Apache village.

For many Western Apaches, the highlight of the year is the White Mountain Apache Tribal Fair and Rodeo, which is held annually in early September, where people get together to take part in a variety of competitions, parades, and a carnival.

THE EASTERN APACHES TODAY

CHAPTER 13

In 1936, the Kiowa-Apaches in western Oklahoma joined with the Kiowas to form a business council for the tribes. Today, the two tribes operate many programs for their people, including health care and educational programs.

Until the 1930s, the Mescalero Apaches of southeastern New Mexico had leased their land for cattle grazing. They then began their own cattle-raising operation, increasing tribal revenue from $18,000 to $101,000 during their first three years. Timber sales also provide tribal income.

In 1963, the Mescaleros bought a nearby ski area. It is now a year-round tourist attraction, with a large hotel, tennis courts, restaurants, and a golf course.

In northern New Mexico, the Jicarilla Apaches discovered oil on their reservation in the 1950s. By the 1990s, tribal revenue from the oil was $11 million a year. Today, there are more than 2,000 oil and gas wells on Jicarilla land.

An Eastern Apache traditional drummer and singer is shown here. The drum is at the very heart of traditional Apache dances.

The Apache population is now increasing and is in the tens of thousands. The survival of their people and their culture is a **testament** to their strength. They still face many problems, but they are facing those challenges and looking to the future with hope for a better life for their people.

GLOSSARY

agile: Able to move quickly and easily.

ally: To unite.

clan: A group of related families.

culture: The arts, beliefs, and customs that form a people's way of life.

drought: A long period of time during which there is very little or no rain.

economy: The way a country or people produces, divides up, and uses its goods and money.

guerrilla warfare: Irregular military actions often carried out by small, independent forces.

hostility: An unfriendly attitude, state, or action.

mobile: Able to move or be moved freely and easily.

reservation: Land set aside by the government for specific Native American tribes to live on.

scholarship: Formal study of a subject.

semiprecious stones: A fairly valuable stone.

significance: The quality of being important.

tepee: A tent that is shaped like a cone and was used in the past by some Native Americans as a house.

terrain: Land of a particular kind.

testament: Proof that something exists or is true.

FOR MORE INFORMATION

BOOKS

Benoit, Peter, and Mark Friedman. *The Apache*. New York, NY: Children's Press, 2011.

Birchfield, D.L., and Helen Dwyer. *Apache History and Culture*. New York, NY: Gareth Stevens Publishing, 2012.

Sanford, William R. *Apache Chief Geronimo*. Berkeley Heights, NJ: Enslow Publishers, Inc., 2013.

WEBSITES

Due to the changing nature of Internet links, PowerKids Press has developed an online list of websites related to the subject of this book. This site is updated regularly. Please use this link to access the list: www.powerkidslinks.com/sona/apa

INDEX